WITH SIGN

International Sign Language 2007

Divided into five Sections to cover the action on:

The Teebox | Fairway | Hazards | Green

and of course the 19th hole.

Editor: Lorna McCormack

Published by Simply Signing Publications
Simply Signing Ltd.,
Tara Winthrop Complex
Nevinstown Lane
Swords
County Dublin
Ireland

GOLF
WITH SIGN

Simply Signing

Published by Simply Signing Publications

Copyright © 2007 by Simply Signing Ltd.
Tara Winthrop Complex
Nevinstown Lane
Swords
County Dublin
Ireland

Tel: +435 (0)1 8907507
Email: info@simplysigning.ie

Editor: Lorna McCormack
Photography & Layout :   Oliver Monks

Photographs on pages 3,34,44,57,79, inside back cover and
top picture front cover courtesy of St. Margaret's Golf and
Country Club.

ISBN 9780955791802

GOLF
WITH SIGN

Simply Signing

International Sign Language
2007

CONTENTS

GOLF
WITH SIGN

Simply Signing

International Sign Language
2007

CONTENTS

 Hazards 44

 The Green 57

 The Clubhouse 67

5

GOLF
WITH SIGN

Simply Signing

International Sign Language
2007

About This Book

For the first time International Sign has been collected into one volume and made available not only to golfers but to the general public.

The signs have been compiled in consultation with the Vice-President of the World Deaf Golf Federation and every effort has been made to conform to common usage.

This book has been designed to enhance communication between Hearing, Hard of Hearing and Deaf Golfers. The illustrated Signs are highly visual depicting the logical progression of the sign through photographs.

This book can also be used as a handy reference for corporate business during multi-lingual golf events.

How to use this book

Because of the visual nature of the illustrations the signs are read from left to right.

The illustrations break the sign down into their various parts allowing us to minimize the use of directional arrows. In fact there are only two occurrences of directional aids, one you will find self-explanatory, and the other one used for Ground Under Repair indicates a tapping motion of the upper hand onto the lower hand.

About Simply Signing

Simply Signing was founded in 2007 By Lorna McCormack with the goal of providing access to Irish Sign Language.

In order to acheive this a number of programmes were designed initally around parents requirements.

As Simply Signing progressed a number of other areas were identified where the use of Irish Sign Language would be benefical.

Significantly, these were in the areas of Health Care and Special needs.

As a result Simply Signing have designed tailor-made programmes which have proved successful in Nursing Homes and Autistic Schools and is currently researching other areas where the use of sign language can overcome communication difficulties.

In October 2007 Simply Signing was delighed to received the 'Highly Commended Award' at the Fingal County Enterprise Awards where the judges described Lorna as a "dedicated educator".

In that spirit Lorna and her husband Geoffrey developed the idea of 'Golf with sign'. Geoffrey is a keen golfer and has represented Ireland many times in the World Deaf Golf Championships

GOLF
WITH SIGN

Simply Signing

International Sign Language
2007

Foreword

This is the 1st edition of 'Golf with sign' and it has been in the making for the past year. During that time we have been fortunate to work with a number of organisations and exceptional golfers and it is due to the experience and inspiration of golfers that this publication has come about.

Golf is played by millions of people throughout the world, many of those Deaf or Hard of Hearing so there has always been a need for a comprehensive book on signs for golf. 'Golf with sign' will help to fill that need, it is a specific guide on how to communicate with your golfing partner, who may have a hearing impairment, and so enhance the friendship created by this sport.

As a user-friendly guide it also offers an alternative means to corporate businesses for overcoming any language barriers during golfing events.

Simply Signing has worked closely with the Irish Deaf Golf Union and Don Conway, Vice President of the World Deaf Golf Federation. The Golf Union of Ireland have also been supportive and encouraging.
The team would like to thank St., Margarets Golf and Country Club for their assistance, in particular, thanks to Carol for finding us the time and space to take the photographs and to Gary Kearney for his advice and suggestions.
Fingal County Enterprise Board have been a great source of guidance throughout the year, their support and advice has helped us realise our ambition to publish 'Golf with sign'

We hope you enjoy the book and find it helpful.

Lorna McCormack

GOLF
WITH SIGN

Simply Signing

International Sign Language
2007

TABLES DES MATIERES.

GOLF
WITH SIGN

Simply Signing

International Sign Language
2007

TABLES DES MATIERES.

Obstacles 44

Le green 57

Le clubhouse 67

GOLF
WITH SIGN

Simply Signing

À propos de ce livre.

Pour la première fois, la langue des signes internationale a été rassemblée en un volume unique disponible non seulement aux golfeurs mais aussi au grand public.
Les signes ont été compilés en consultation avec le vice-président de la Fédération mondiale de golf des Sourds, et beaucoup d'efforts ont été faits afin de se conformer à l'usage commun.

Ce livre a été conçu afin d'améliorer la communication entre les golfeurs entendants, malentendants et sourds. Les signes illustrés sont extrême-ment visuels et représentent la progression logique du signe à travers des photos.

Ce livre peut également servir de référence pratique pour les sociétés lors de tournois multilingues de golf.

Comment utiliser ce livre.

En raison de la nature visuelle des illustrations, les signes se lisent de gauche à droite.

Les illustrations décomposent le signe en plusieurs parties, ce qui nous permet de réduire l'utilisation de flèches directionnelles. Les aides directionnelles ne sont en fait utilisées que deux fois : l'une d'elle se passe d'explication, et l'autre, utilisée pour Terrain en réparation, indique un mouvement de tapotement de la main du dessus sur la main du dessous.

À propos de Simply Signing.

Simply Signing a été crée en 2007 par Lorna McCormack, dans le but de rendre la langue des signes irlandaise plus accessible.

Afin d'atteindre cet objectif, un certain nombre de programmes ont été initialement conçus autour des besoins de parents.

Lorsque Simply Signing a commencé à se développer, d'autres domaines au sein desquels l'utilisation de la langue des signes irlandaise pourrait être utile ont été identifiés.

Les domaines les plus significa-tifs étaient ceux de la santé et des besoins particuliers.
Simply Signing a par conséquent conçu des programmes sur mesure qui se sont révélés être une vraie réussite dans les maisons de repos et les écoles pour enfants autistes, et est actuellement à la recherche d'autres domaines au sein desquels la langue des signes peut aider à surmonter des problèmes de communication.

En octobre 2007, Simply Signing a été fier de recevoir le 'Highly Commended Award' aux Fingal County Enterprise Awards, cérémonie pendant laquelle les juges ont qualifié Lorna d'« éducatrice dévouée ».
C'est dans cet esprit que Lorna et son mari Geoffrey ont développé l'idée du 'golf avec les signes'.
Geoffrey est un golfeur enthousiaste qui a représenté l'Irlande plus d'une fois lors des Championnats mondiaux de golf des Sourds.

International Sign Language 2007

Avant-propos

Ceci est la première édition de Le golf avec les signes, qui a été développé au cours de l'année passée. Pendant cette période, nous avons eu la chance de travailler conjointement avec un certain nombre d'organisations et de golfeurs exceptionnels, et c'est grâce à l'expérience et l'inspiration de ces golfeurs que cette publication a vu le jour.

Des millions de personnes à travers le monde jouent au golf, et beaucoup d'entre eux sont malentendants ou sourds. Le besoin d'un livre complet sur les signes a donc toujours été présent. L'objectif de Le golf avec les signes est de répondre à ce besoin. C'est un guide spécifique qui vous explique comment communiquer avec un partenaire de golf qui est malentendant et qui vous permet de renforcer votre amitié grâce à ce sport.

C'est un guide facile d'emploi qui peut également offrir d'autres moyens de communications aux sociétés afin de les aider à surmonter les barrières de langue lors de tournois de golf.

Simply Signing a travaillé conjointement avec le syndicat de golf des Sourds irlandais ainsi que Don Conway, le vice-président de la Fédération mondiale de golf des Sourds. La fédération de golf d'Irlande a également offert son soutien et ses encouragements.

L'équipe souhaite remercier le club de golf et de loisirs de St. Margaret pour son aide, et en particulier Carol, pour avoir pris le temps et trouver les lieux pour prendre les photos, ainsi que Gary Kearney pour ses conseils et suggestions.

Le Fingal County Enterprise Board a été une source importance de conseils tout au long de l'année. Leurs soutien et conseils nous ont aidé à réaliser à notre ambition de publier Le golf avec les signes.

Nous espérons que vous apprécierez ce livre et qu'il vous sera utile.

Lorna McCormack

GOLF
WITH SIGN

Simply Signing

International Sign Language
2007

INHALT.

International Sign Language
2007

Inhalt.

GOLF
WITH SIGN

Simply Signing

Über dieses Buch.

Zum ersten mal wurde eine internationale Gebärdensprache in einem einzelnem Band zusammengestellt und steht damit nicht nur Golfern, sondern auch der allgemein interessierten Öffentlichkeit zur Verfügung. Die vorliegenden Gebärden wurden in Beratung mit dem Vizepräsidenten der World Deaf Golf Federation zusammengestellt und es wurde keine Mühe gescheut, sie der allgemein gebräuchlichen Nutzung der Gebärdensprache anzugleichen.

Dieses Buch wurde erstellt, um die Kommunikation zwischen hörenden, schwerhörigen und tauben Golfern zu erleichtern. Die illustrierten Gebärden werden bildhaft dargestellt und in ihrer logischen Abfolge durch Fotos beschrieben.

Dieses Buch kann auch bei mehrsprachigen geschäftlichen Besprechungen während Golfveranstaltungen als nützliche Referenz benutzt werden.

Praktische Anwendung des Buches

Die Reihenfolge der dargestellten Gebärden ist von links nach rechts.

Die Illustrationen schlüsseln die einzelnen Gebärden in ihre einzelnen Bewegungen auf, was es uns ermöglichte, auf Richtungspfeile beinahe komplett zu verzichten. Tatsächlich gibt es nur zwei Bilder, in denen Richtungsanweisungen verwendet werden. Eine davon is ist selbsterklärend, die andere wurde für „Bereich in Reparatur" benutzt. Der richtungsweisende Pfeil zeigt eine klopfende Bewegung der oberen Hand auf die untere Hand.

Über Simply Signing.

Simply Signing wurde 2007 von Lorna McCormack mit dem Ziel gegründet, anderen Zugang zu der Irischen Gebärdensprache zu geben.

Um dieses zu erreichen, wurden zunächst Programme geschaffen, die sich mit für Eltern notwendigen Gebärden beschäftigten.

Während des Entwicklungsprozesses von Simply Signing wurden auch andere Bereiche identifiziert, in denen die Kenntnis der Irischen Gebärdensprache von Nutzen sein konnte.

Bedeutsam war diese Notwendigkeit im Gesundheitswesen und im Bereich der Behindertenbetreuung. Als Resultat hat Simply Signing maßgeschneiderte Programme entwickelt, die sich hervorragend in Pflegeheimen und Schulen für autistische Kinder bestens bewährt haben. Gegenwärtig werden andere Bereiche erforscht, in welchen die Nutzung einer Gebärdensprache Kommunikationsschwierigkeiten aus dem Weg räumen könnten..

Im October 2007 wurde den hocherfreuten Schöpfern von Simply Signing die Auszeichnung ‚Höchst Empfehlenswert' der „Fingal County Enterprise Awards" verliehen. Die Preisrichter beschrieben Lorna als eine „engagierte Erzieherin"

In diesem Sinne haben Lorna und ihr Mann Geoffrey die Idee von „Golf mit Gebärden" entwickelt.. Geoffrey ist ein begeisterter Golfer und hat Irland oft in den World Deaf Golf Championships vertreten.

International Sign Language
2007

Vorwort.

Dies ist die erste Ausgabe von „Golf mit Gebärden" und wurde im letzten Jahr zusammengestellt. Während dieser Zeit hatten wir das Glück, mit einer Anzahl von Organisationen und außergewöhnlichen Golfern zusammenarbeiten zu können, und Dank der Erfahrung und der Inspiration dieser Menschen können wir dieses Buch jetzt veröffentlichen.

Golf wird von Millionen von Menschen weltweit gespielt und viele Spieler sind taub oder schwerhörig. Deshalb besteht seit Langem der Bedarf nach einem umfangreichem Buch, welches die Gebärden für Golf beschreibt.

Als benutzerfreundlicher Führer bietet dieses Buch auch eine Alternative für Geschäftsgespräche während Golfveranstaltungen, um eventuelle Sprachbarrieren zu überwinden.

Simply Signing hat eng mit der Irish Deaf Golf Union und Don Conway, dem Vizepräsidenten der World Deaf Golf Federation, zusammengearbeitet. Die Golf Union of Ireland war ebenfalls sehr hilfsbereit und unterstützend.
Das Team möchte ebenfalls dem St. Margaret's Golf and Country Club für seine Hilfe und Unterstützung danken, vor allem Carol, die Zeit und Platz für uns gefunden hat, Fotos zu machen. Danke auch an Gary Kearney für seinen Rat und seine Vorschläge.
Das Fingal County Enterprise Board war für uns das ganze Jahr hindurch eine großartige Quelle für Ratschläge, ihre Unterstützung und ihre Hinweise haben uns geholfen, „Golf mit Gebärden" zu veröffentlichen.

Wir hoffen, dass Sie das Buch genießen und als hilfreich empfinden werden.

Lorna McCormack

GOLF
WITH SIGN

Simply Signing

International Sign Language
2007

CONTENIDOS.

GOLF
WITH SIGN

Simply **S**igning

International Sign Language
2007

CONTENIDOS.

GOLF
WITH SIGN

$\mathcal{S}$imply $\mathcal{S}$igning

Acerca de este libro.

Por primera vez, el Lenguaje de Señas Internacional ha sido recopilado en un volumen y puesto a la disposición, no sólo de los golfistas, sino del público en general.
Las señas han sido compiladas en consultoría con el Vicepresidente de la Federación Mundial de Golfistas Sordos, y se ha hecho todo el esfuerzo posible para reflejar las señales de uso común.

Éste libro ha sido diseñado para mejorar la comunicación entre Golfistas con Audición no Impedida, Golfistas con Sordera Parcial y Golfistas con Sordera Total. Las Señas ilustradas son altamente visuales, demostrando la progresión lógica de las señas mediante fotografías.

Éste libro también puede ser utilizado como una referencia útil para las empresas comerciales durante los eventos del golf multilingüe.

Como utilizar este libro.

A causa de la naturaleza visual de las ilustraciones, las señas se leen de izquierda a derecha.

Las ilustraciones dividen la seña en sus distintas partes, permitiendo minimizar el uso de flechas direccionales. De hecho, sólo hay dos ocurrencias de ayudas direccionales, una que será innecesario explicar, y la otra, utilizada para Terreno Bajo Reparaciones, indica una moción de golpecitos con la mano superior sobre la mano inferior.

Acerca de Simply Signing (Señas Sencillas).

Simply Signing fue fundada en 2007 por Lorna McCormack, con la meta de proveer acceso al Lenguaje de Señas Irlandés.

Para lograr esto, varios programas fueron diseñados inicialmente en torno a los requisitos de los padres.

a medida que progresó Simply Signing, otras áreas fueron identificadas en donde el uso del Lenguaje de Señas Irlandés sería beneficioso.

,De modo significativo, éstas estaban en las áreas de Cuidado Médico y Necesidades Especiales.
Como resultado, Simply Signing ha diseñado programas personalizados que han probado su eficacia en hogares de cuidado de ancianos y escuelas para alumnos autistas, y actualmente está investigando otras áreas donde el uso del lenguaje de señas puede sobrepasar las dificultades de comunicación.

En octubre de 2007, Simply Signing tuvo el placer de recibir el "Premio Altamente Condecorado" en las Premiaciones a Empresarios del Condado de Fingal, donde los jueces describieron a Lorna como una "educadora dedicada". En ese espíritu, Lorna y su marido Geoffrey desarrollaron la idea del "Lenguaje de Señas para el Juego de Golf". Geoffrey es un excelente golfista y ha representado a Irlanda varias veces en varios Campeonatos Mundiales de Golfistas Sordos

GOLF
WITH SIGN

Simply Signing

International Sign Language
2007

Prefacio.

Ésta es la primera edición de "Lenguaje de Señas para el Juego de Golf", y ha estado en desarrollo durante el año pasado. Durante ese tiempo, hemos sido afortunados en trabajar con un número de organizaciones y golfistas excepcionales, y gracias a la experiencia e inspiración de estos golfistas que esta publicación ha sido posible.

El golf es jugado por millones de personas a través del mundo, muchas de ellas padeciendo de sordera o sordera parcial, de modo que siempre ha existido la necesidad de un libro comprensivo sobre señas para el golf. "Lenguaje de Señas para el Juego de Golf" ayudará a suplir esa necesidad al ser una guía específica para comunicarse con su compañero de golf, que puede tener un impedimento auditivo, y así mejorar la amistad creada por este deporte.

Al ser una guía enfocada en ayudar al usuario, también ofrece un medio alternativo para que las empresas comerciales se sobrepongan a cualquier barrera del lenguaje durante los eventos de golf.

Simply Signing ha trabajado de forma cercana con la Unión de Golfistas Sordos de Irlanda y con Don Conway, Vicepresidente de la Federación Mundial de Golfistas Sordos. La Unión Irlandesa del Golf también nos ha provisto apoyo y motivación.
El equipo desea agradecer al St., Margaret's Golf and Country Club por su ayuda, y en particular, gracias a Carol por encontrarnos el tiempo y espacio para tomar las fotografías, y a Gary Kearney por su asesoría y sugerencias.

La Junta de Empresarios del Condado de Fingal ha sido una gran fuente de asesoría durante el año, y su apoyo y asesoría nos ha ayudado a fomentar nuestra ambición de publicar "Lenguaje de Señas para el Juego de Golf".

Esperamos que usted disfrute de esta publicación, y que le ayude en los fines para la cual está redactada.

Lorna McCormack

Green Golf Ball

don't lose it!

www.greengolfball.com

Your One Stop Shop for Irish Golf

We offer:

Golfing Packages
Hotel Reservations
Green Fees
Transport
Car Hire
Local knowledge
For all your Irish Golfing Requirements –
you will not get better value!

Greengolfball Ltd

Tel: 00 353 1 843 5570

Fax: 00 353 1 808 5669

info@greengolfball.com

www.greengolfball.com

Hire a Trolley
Louer un chariot
Einen Trolley mieten.
Rentar un Carrito.

Hire a Buggy
Louer une voiturette
Einen Buggy mieten.
Rentar un Buggy.

Front Nine
Premier neuf
Front nine.
Primeros nueve.

Back Nine
Deuxième neuf.
Back Nine.
Nueve posteriores.

The Tee Box.
Départ
Der Abschlag.
La caja de Tee.

Tee-Box
Départ
Tee Box.
.Caja de saque

White
Blanc
Weiß
Blanco

Blue
Bleu
Blau
Azul

Yellow
Jaune
Gelb
Amarillo

Red
Rouge
Rot
Rojo

Ball to the left
Balle vers la gauche
Ball zur Linken.
Bola a la izquierda.

Golf with sign

Ball to the right
Balle vers la droite
Ball zur Rechten.
Bola a la derecha.

Third Shot
Troisième coup
Dritter Schlag.
Tercer tiro.

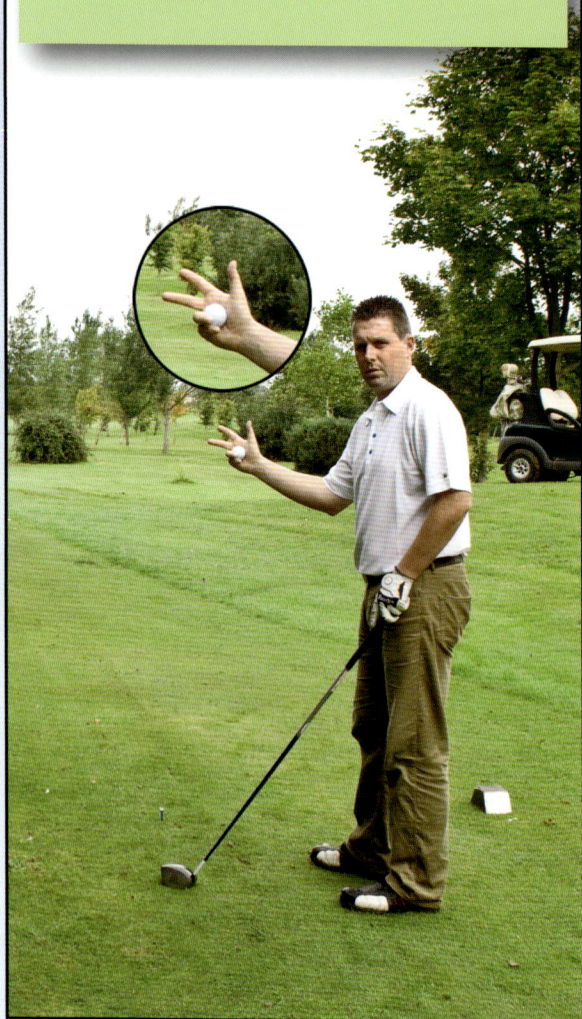

Provisional Ball
Balle provisoire
Provisorischer Ball.
Bola provisional.

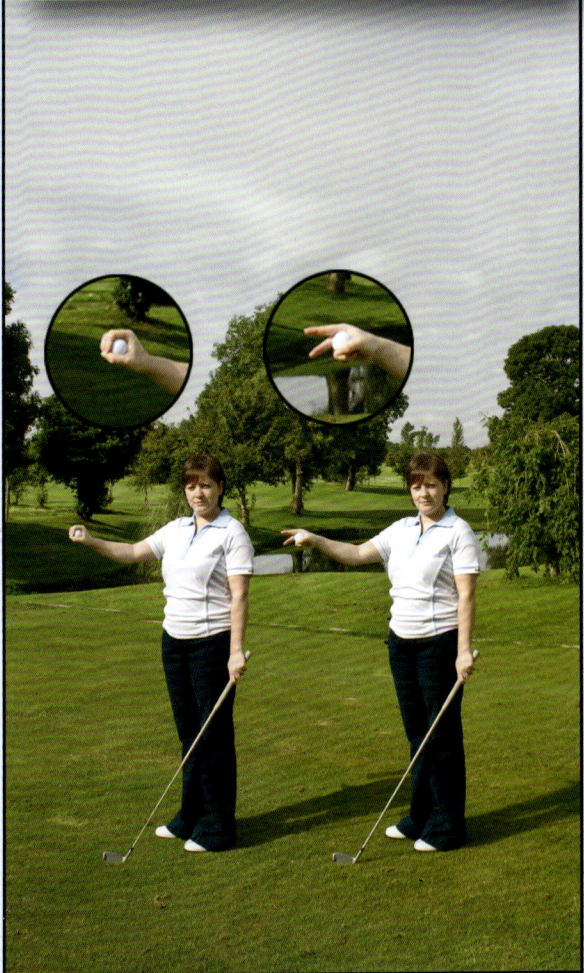

Your Turn
À votre tour
Sie sind dran.
Su turno.

Good Shot
Bon coup
Ein guter Schlag.
Buen tiro.

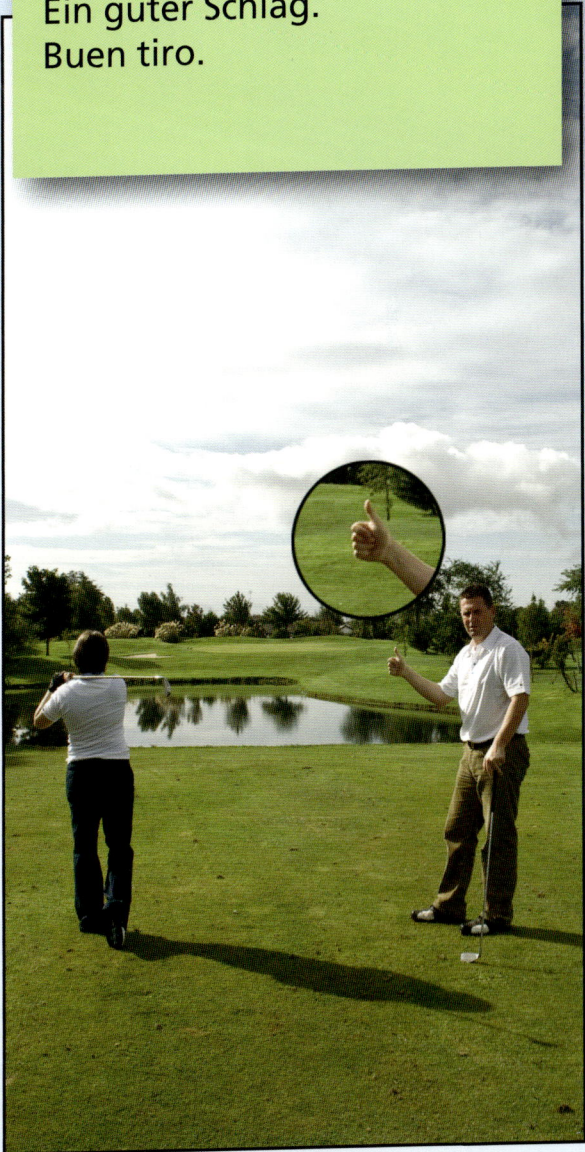

The Fairway.
L'allée
Der Fairway.
La grama.

Ball on the fairway
Balle sur le fairway
Ball auf dem Fairway.
Bola en terreno abierto.

Ball in left bunker
Balle dans le bunker de gauche
Ball im linken Bunker.
Bola en banco izquierdo.

Ball in right bunker
Balle dans le bunker de droite
Ball im rechten Bunker.
Bola en banco derecho.

Out of Bounds
Hors limite
Ball im Aus/Out of Bounds.
Fuera de los límites.

Trees
Arbres
Bäume.
Árboles.

Bushes
Buissons
Büsche.
Arbustos.

Placing everywhere
Placer partout
Den Ball platzieren – egal wo.
Colocar en todos lados.

Lift, Clean and Drop in Rough.
Soulever, nettoyer et déposer dans le rough
Aufheben, Säubern und im Rough fallenlassen.
Levantar, limpiar y dejar en el terreno.

Placing the Ball on Fairway
Placer la balle sur le fairway
Den Ball auf dem Fairway
plazieren.
Colocar la bola en el terreno.

Hazards.
Obstacles
Hindernisse.
Peligros.

Staked tree
Bosquet d'arbres
Gestützter Baum.
Golpeó un árbol.

Free
Libre
Frei.
Libre.

Drop within one club length
Drop à une longueur de club
Innerhalb einer Schlägerlänge
fallenlassen.
Dejar caer en la longitud
de un palo.

Lateral Water Hazard
Obstacle d'eau latéral
Seitliches Wasserhindernis.
Peligro de agua lateral.

One Penalty
Une pénalité
Ein Strafpunkt.
Una penalidad.

Drop
Drop.
Fallenlassen.
Dejar caer.

Two Club Lengths
Longueur de deux clubs.
Zwei Schlägerlängen.
Dos longitudes del palo.

Yellow Stake, One Penalty
Une pénalité au piquet jaune
Gelbe Markierung, eine Strafe
Una penalidad por golpe
amarillo.

Drop
Déposer
Fallenlassen
Dejar caer.

Ground under Repair
Terrain en réparation.
Bereich in Reparatur.
Terreno Bajo Reparaciones.

GROUND
UNDER REPAIR

Free
Libre
Frei.
Libre.

Drop within one club length
Drop à une longueur de club.
Innerhalb einer Schlägerlänge
fallenlassen.
Dejar caer en la longitud de
un palo.

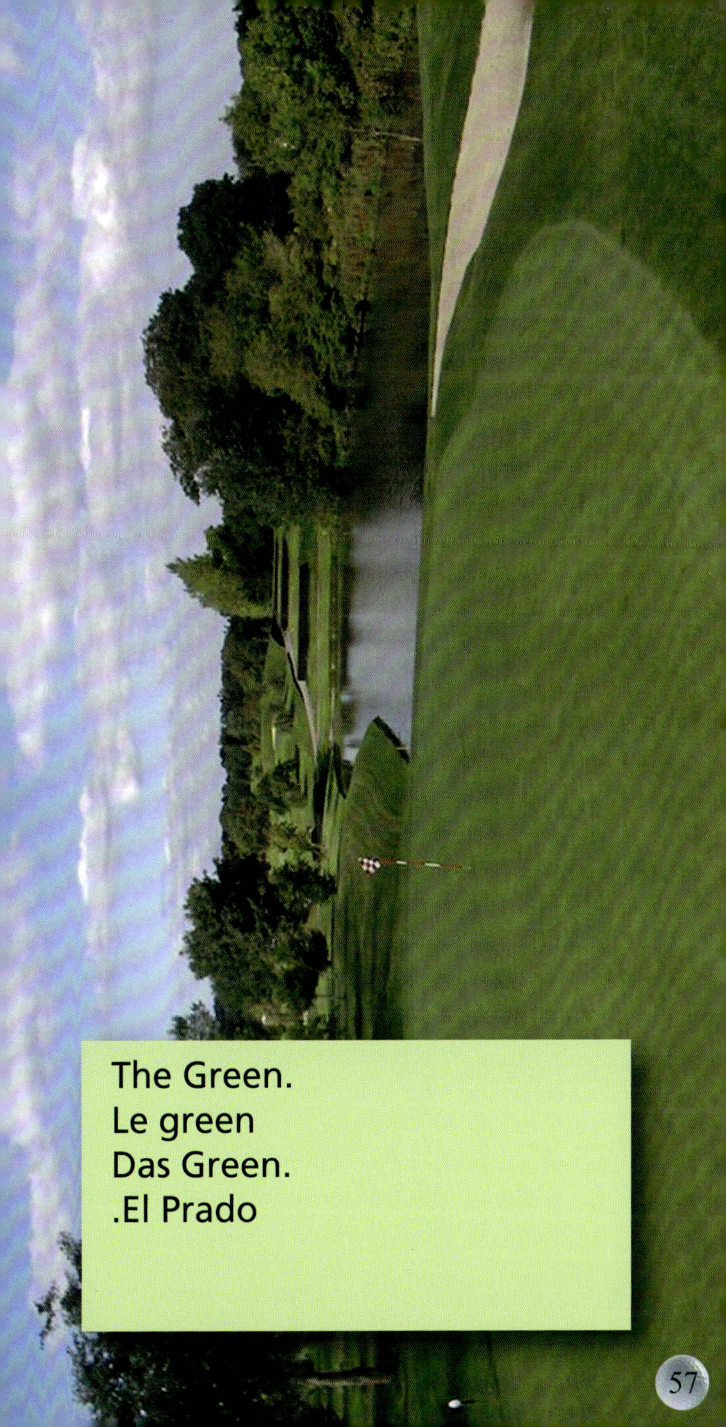

The Green.
Le green
Das Green.
.El Prado

Ball on fringe
Balle sur la zone limite
Ball am Rand.
Bola en el borde.

Ball on Green
Balle sur le green.
Ball auf dem Grün.
Bola en la grama.

G⊕lf with sign

Marking ball on Green
Balle de repère sur le green.
Dem Ball am Green markieren.
Marcar bola en la grama.

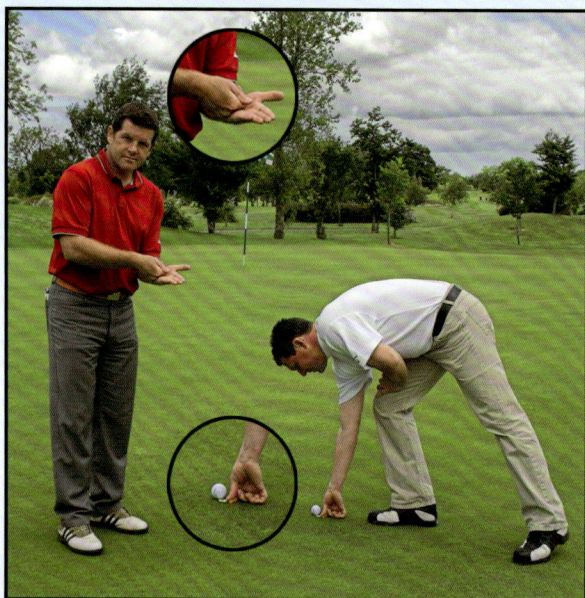

Flag Up
Drapeau tenu levé
Flagge hoch/Flag up.
Bandera arriba.

G⚬lf with sign

Ball in the Hole
Balle dans le trou
Ball im Loch.
Bola en el hoyo.

Green Repair
Réparation du green
Grün wird repariert.
Reparación de grama.

Rule
Règle
Regel.
Regla.

Book
Livre
Buch.
Libro.

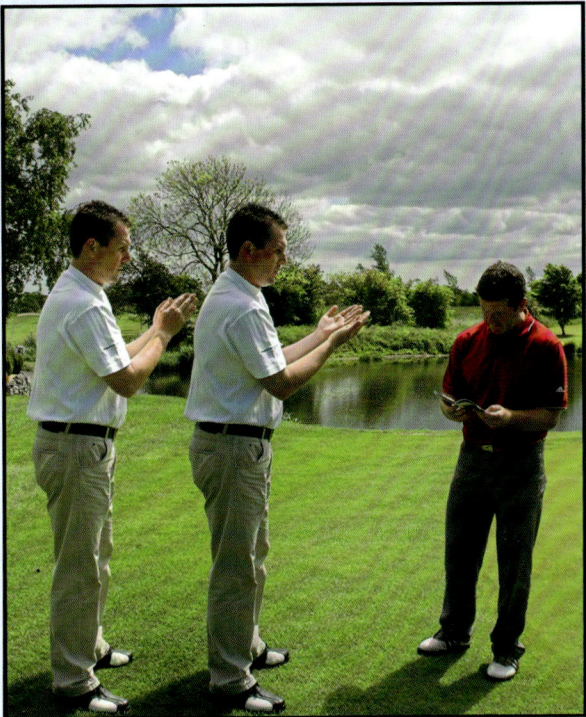

G⛳lf with sign

Scorecard
Feuille de score.
Punktekarte/Score Card.
Tarjeta de puntuación.

The Clubhouse
Le clubhouse
Das Clubhaus.
La casa del club.

Shower
Douche
Dusche.
Ducha.

Towel
Serviette
Handtuch.
Toalla.

Drink
Boisson
Getränk.
Bebida.

Beer
Bière
Bier.
Cerveza.

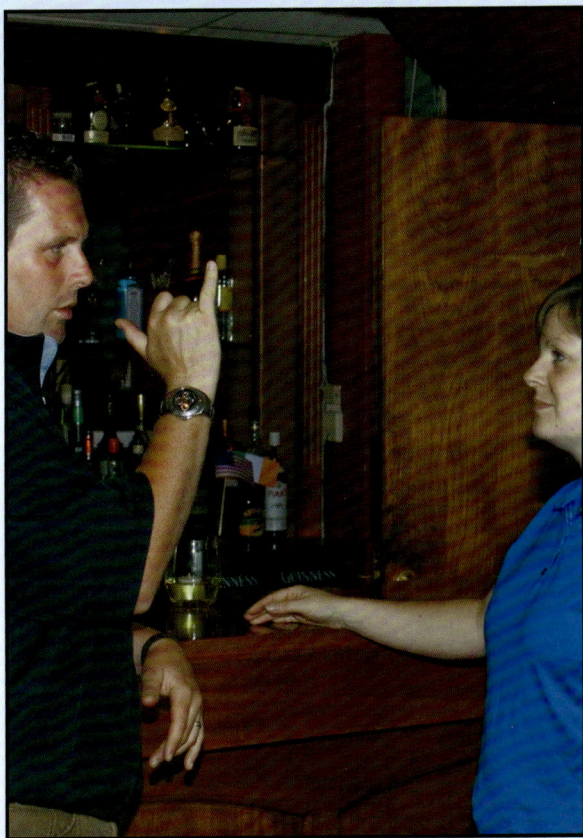

Good Game
Bon jeu
Ein gutes Spiel.
Buen juego.

Bad Game
Mauvais jeu
Ein schlechtes Spiel.
Mal juego.

Food
Nourriture
Essen.
Comida.

Menu
Menu
Menu
Menú

Toilets
Toilettes
Toiletten.
Inodoros.

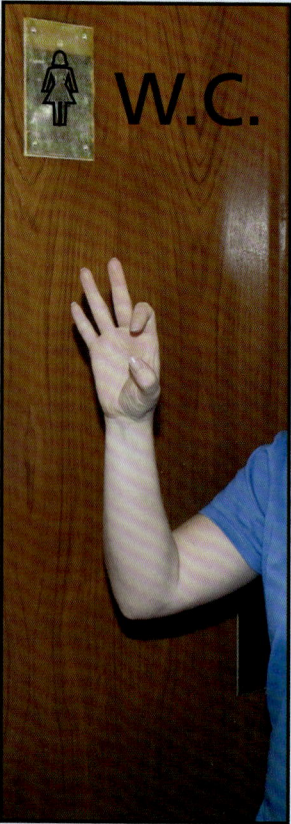

Paybill
Payer l'addition
Die Rechnung bezahlen.
Pagar cuenta.